THE SHEPHERDS SHOOK IN THEIR SHOES

Luke 2 for Children

Written by Michelle Medlock Adams

Illustrated by Dana Regan

CONCORDIA PUBLISHING HOUSE · SAINT LOUIS

One night while shepherds did their jobs
And watched their sheep with care,
An angel of the Lord appeared
And gave them quite a scare!

The shepherds' hearts were full of fear.
They shook right in their shoes!
But then the angel called to them,
"Fear not, I've got good news!"

The shepherds didn't speak a word.
The sheep were quiet too.
They tried to "fear not" like he said,
But that was hard to do.

The angel was extremely bright—
Just like the noonday sun.
And when he spoke, his words of peace
Swept over everyone.

The shepherds listened carefully
To what he had to say.
Somehow they knew deep in their hearts,
It was a holy day.

The angel spoke of Jesus,
The One they'd waited for.
They moved a little closer in.
They wanted to hear more.

“For unto you this day is born
A Savior, Christ the Lord.”
The angel spoke with strength and might.
He could not be ignored.

“He’s in the City of David,”
They heard the angel say.
And then one shepherd said aloud,
“I must go there today!”

“And this shall be a sign to you,”
The angel boldly said.
“You’ll find the babe in swaddling clothes
Upon a small straw bed.”

With that, the angel spoke no more.
Then guess what filled the sky?
It was a multitude of hosts,
All hovering nearby!

The angels came to praise the Lord.
They all began to sing.
"Glory to God in the Highest!"
It was an awesome thing.

Their voices were quite beautiful.
They sang for quite a while:
"Peace on earth, good will toward men."
That made the shepherds smile.

Then suddenly, the angels left.
Their job that night was through.
They had announced the glorious news,
And now the shepherds knew.

"To Bethlehem!" one shepherd said.
"We have to go tonight!"
They longed to praise the King of kings
And see the holy sight.

The shepherds hurried on their way
Until they found the place.
They could not wait to see the Child
And gaze upon His face.

And then at last, they saw the Babe.
Their hearts were filled with joy.
They knew He was the precious Christ—
Not just a baby boy.

The shepherds left the holy place
And shared the news abroad.
They said, “We saw the King of kings!
We saw the Son of God!”

And some who heard the shepherds' news
Were puzzled at each word,
But all the shepherds praised the Lord
For what they'd seen and heard.

They knew they'd seen the King of kings.
They knew it in their heart.
They knew they'd never be the same.
They had a brand-new start.

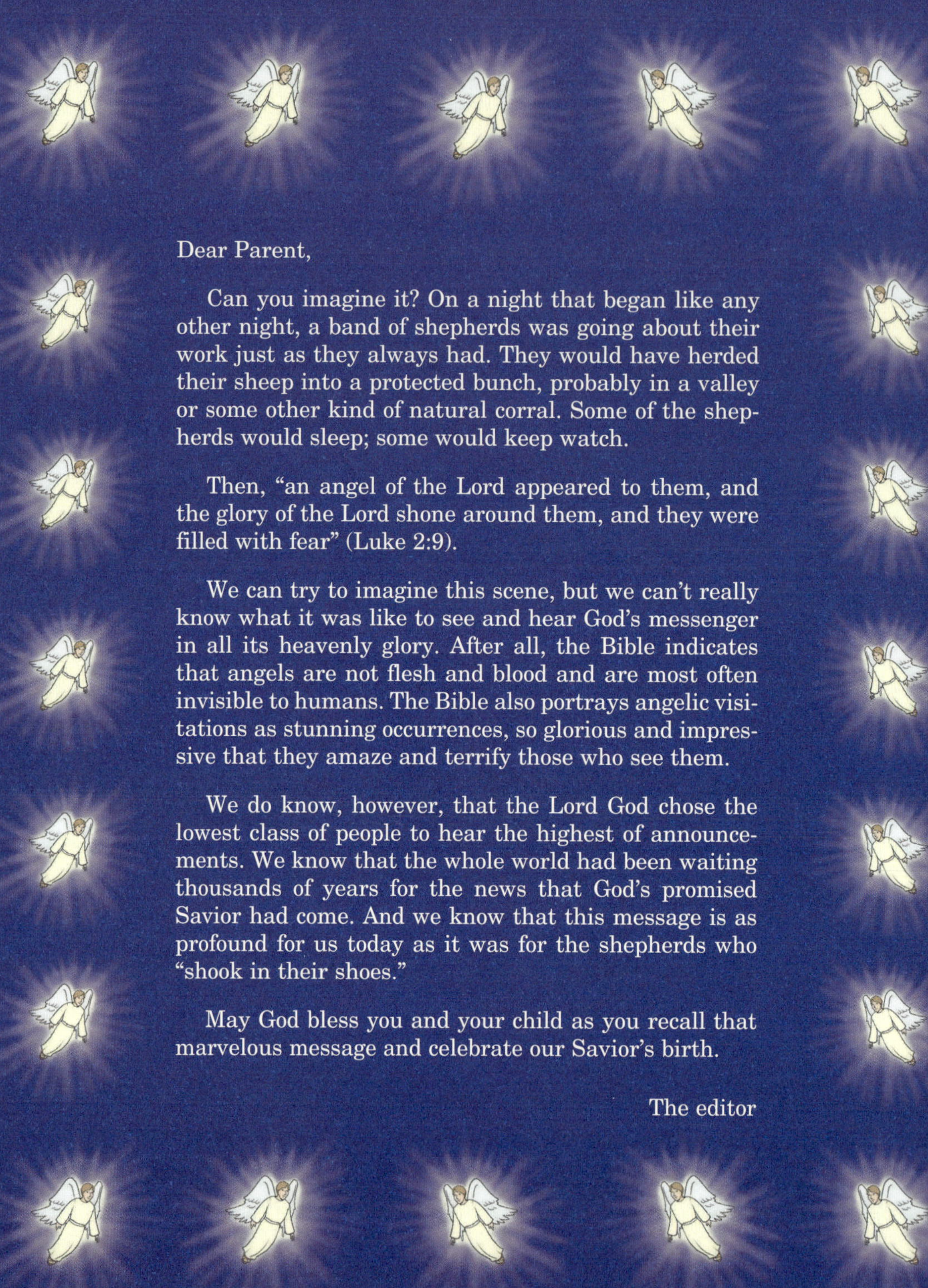

Dear Parent,

Can you imagine it? On a night that began like any other night, a band of shepherds was going about their work just as they always had. They would have herded their sheep into a protected bunch, probably in a valley or some other kind of natural corral. Some of the shepherds would sleep; some would keep watch.

Then, "an angel of the Lord appeared to them, and the glory of the Lord shone around them, and they were filled with fear" (Luke 2:9).

We can try to imagine this scene, but we can't really know what it was like to see and hear God's messenger in all its heavenly glory. After all, the Bible indicates that angels are not flesh and blood and are most often invisible to humans. The Bible also portrays angelic visitations as stunning occurrences, so glorious and impressive that they amaze and terrify those who see them.

We do know, however, that the Lord God chose the lowest class of people to hear the highest of announcements. We know that the whole world had been waiting thousands of years for the news that God's promised Savior had come. And we know that this message is as profound for us today as it was for the shepherds who "shook in their shoes."

May God bless you and your child as you recall that marvelous message and celebrate our Savior's birth.

The editor